This Coloring Book Belongs To:

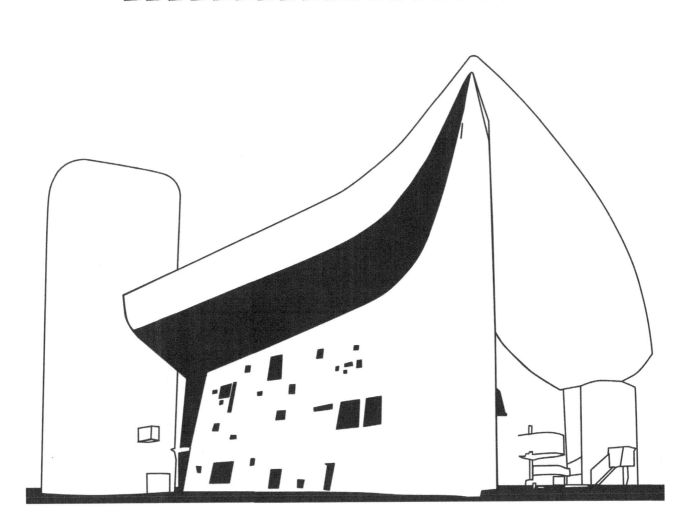

Coloring Book with city architecture

Copyright Architecture Coloring Book

autor, illustrator: Jacek Lasa,

Colorful Houses in Trondheim

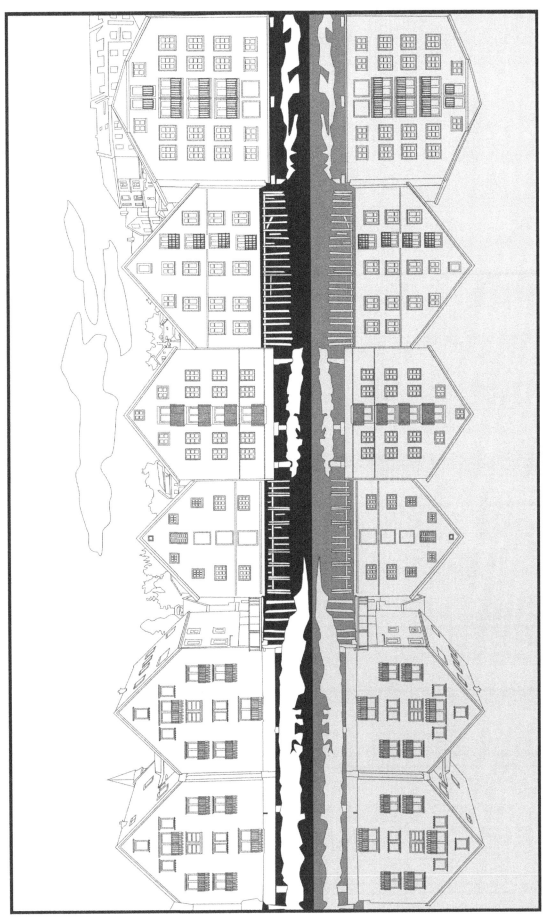

New York

Prowanse - France

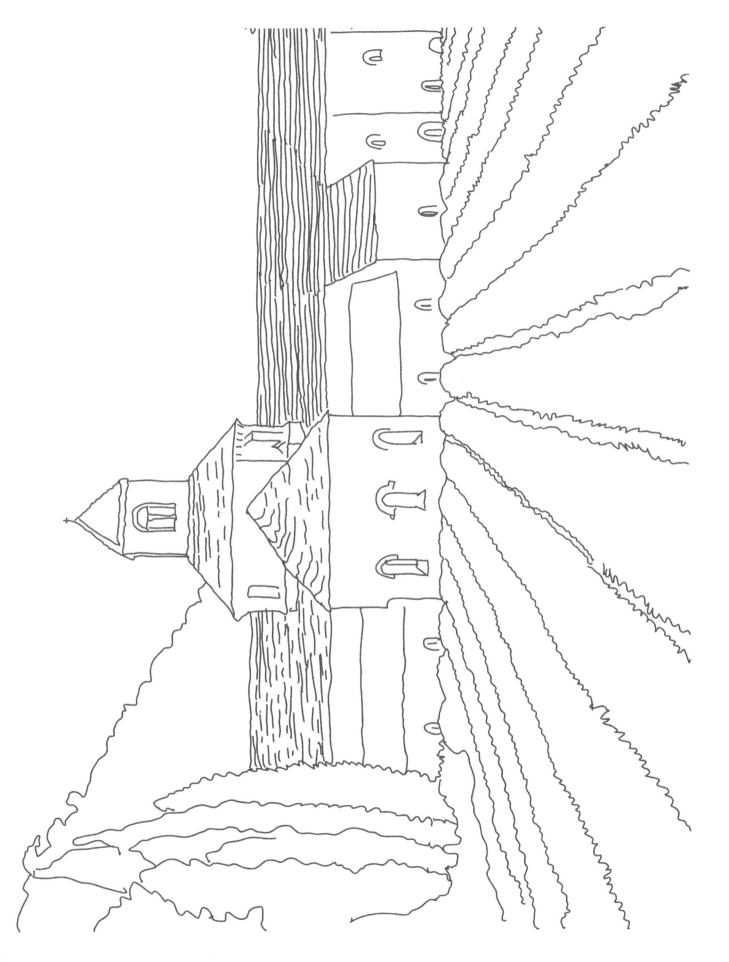

Eiffel Tower

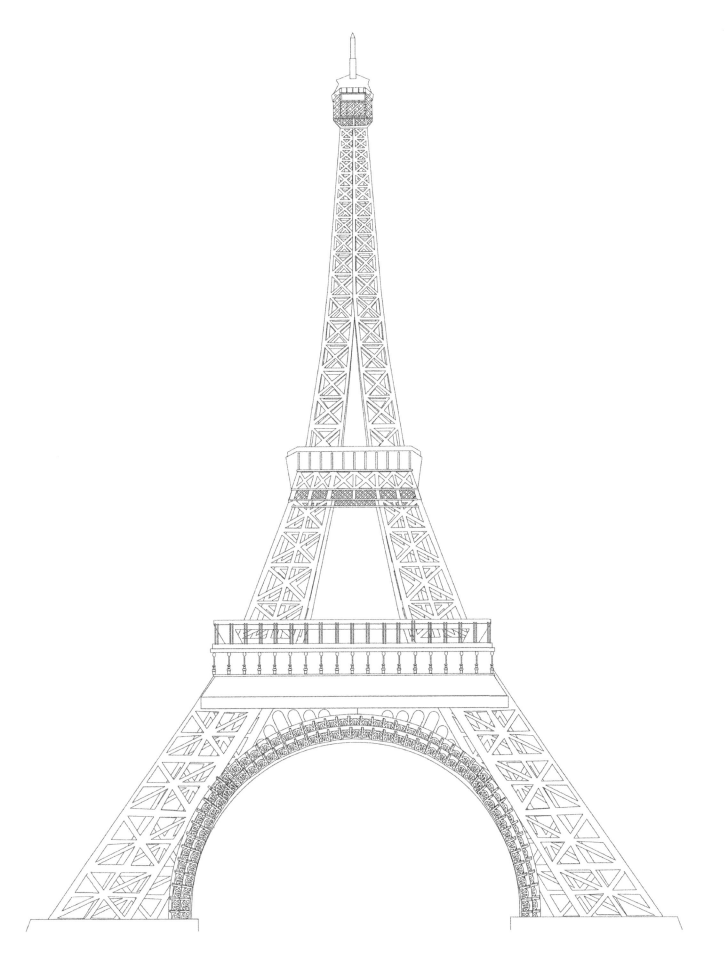

Big Ben

Big Ben

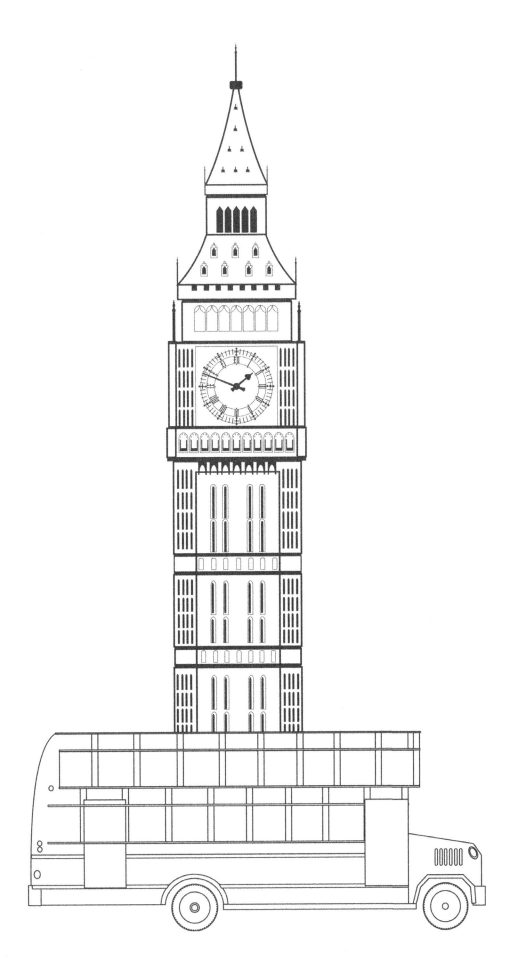

Eiffel Tower

Rialto - Venice

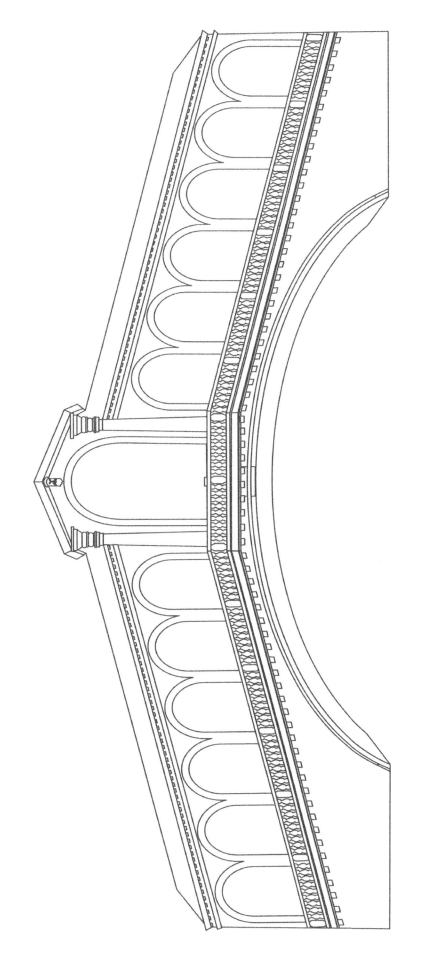

venetian mask

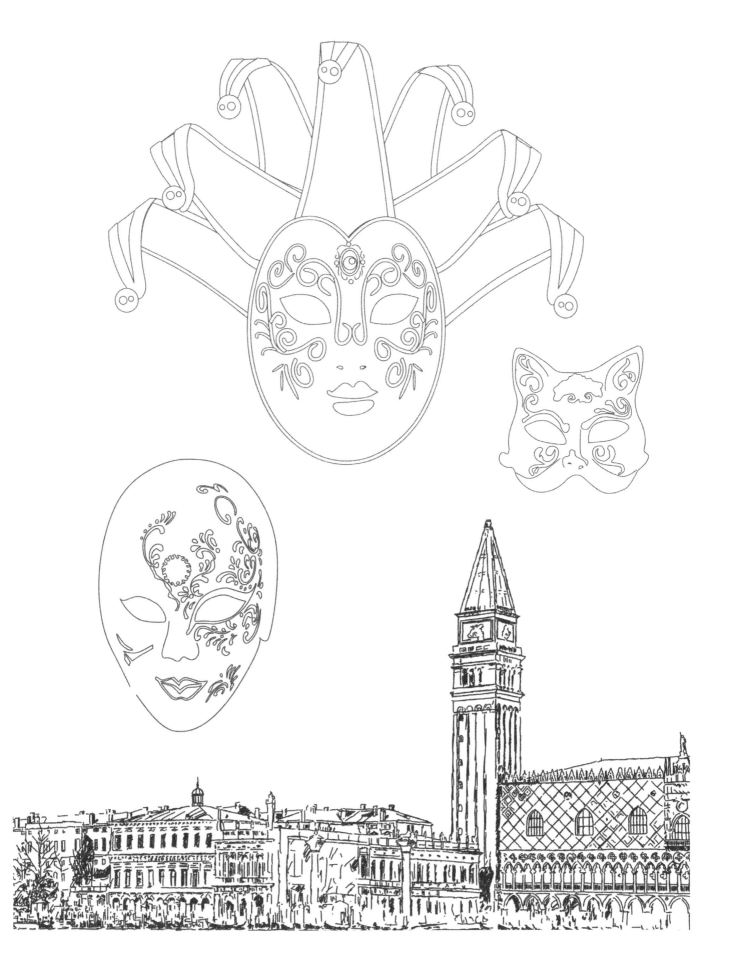

Le Corbusier, Ronchamp Chapel

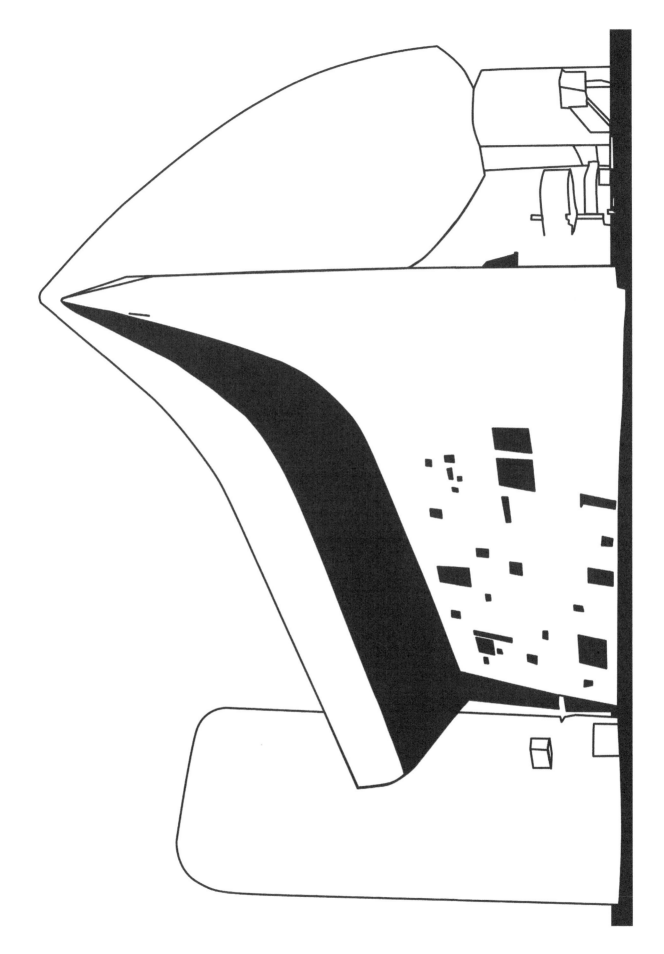

Amsterdam

Amsterdam

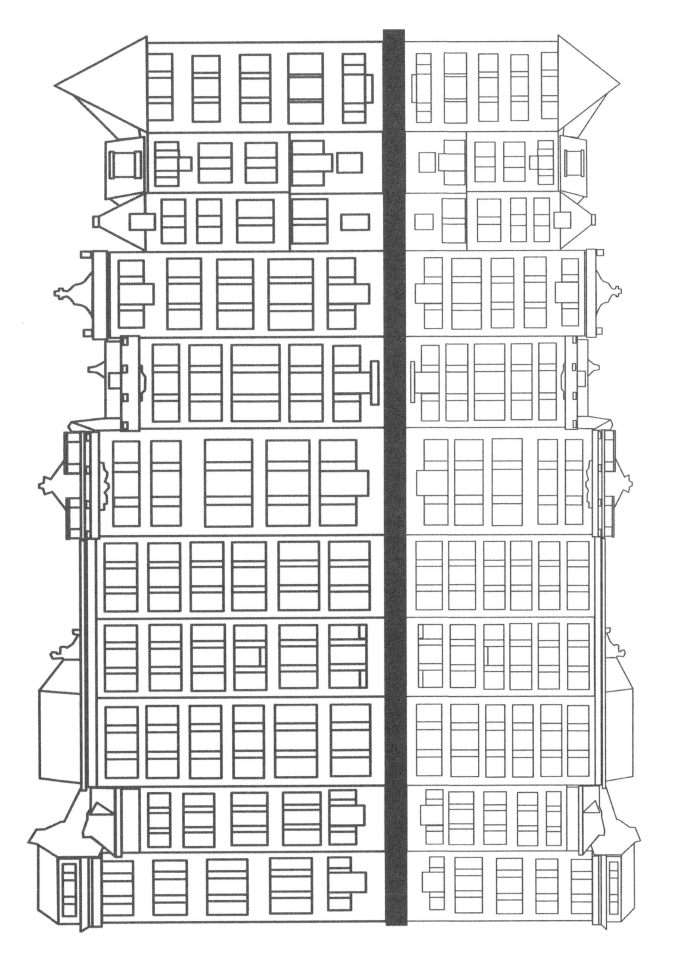

Sydney Opera House

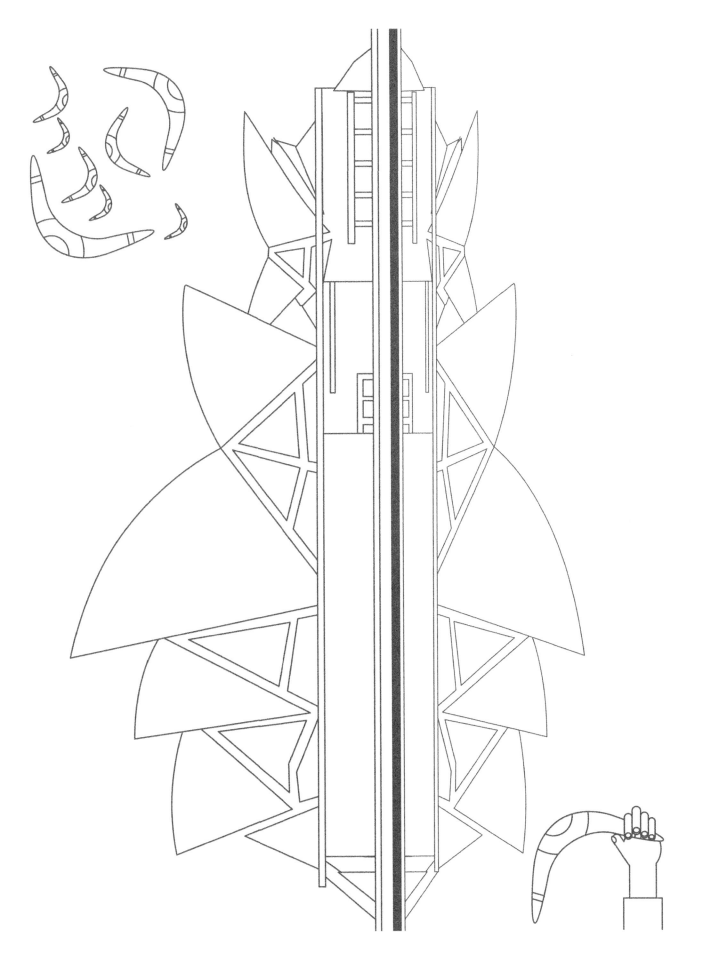

Sevilla

New York

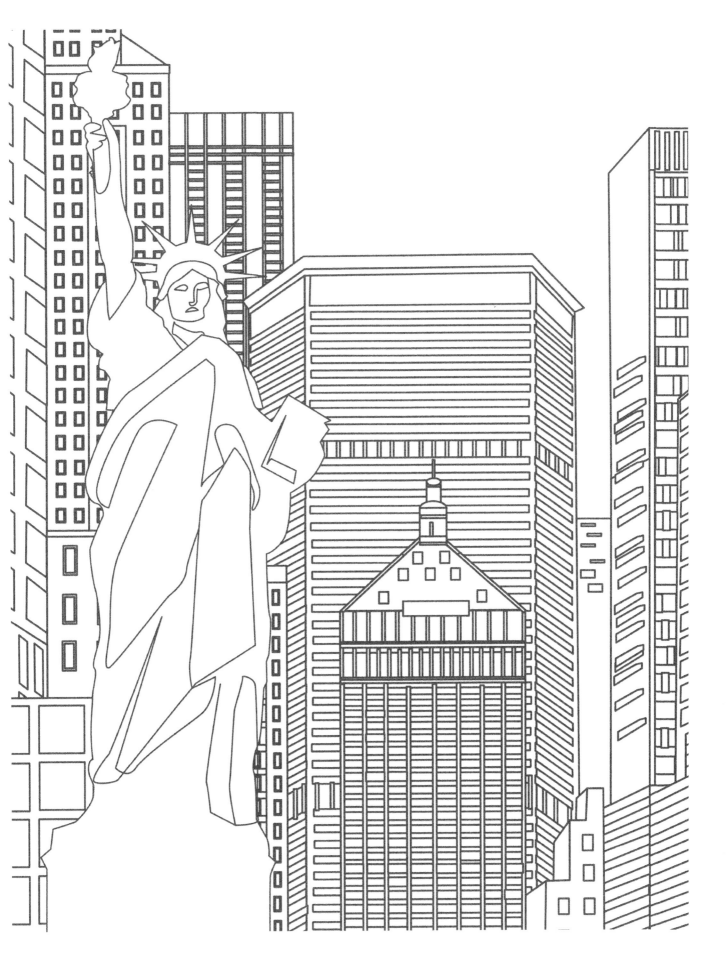

Greek building

Venice

The Colosseum in Rome

Route 66

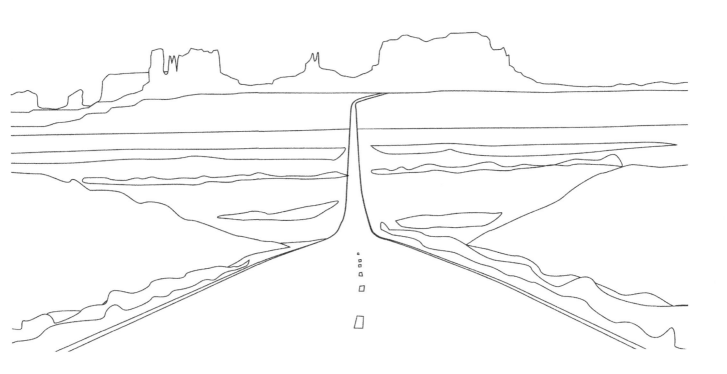

Moscow

Greek style in architecture

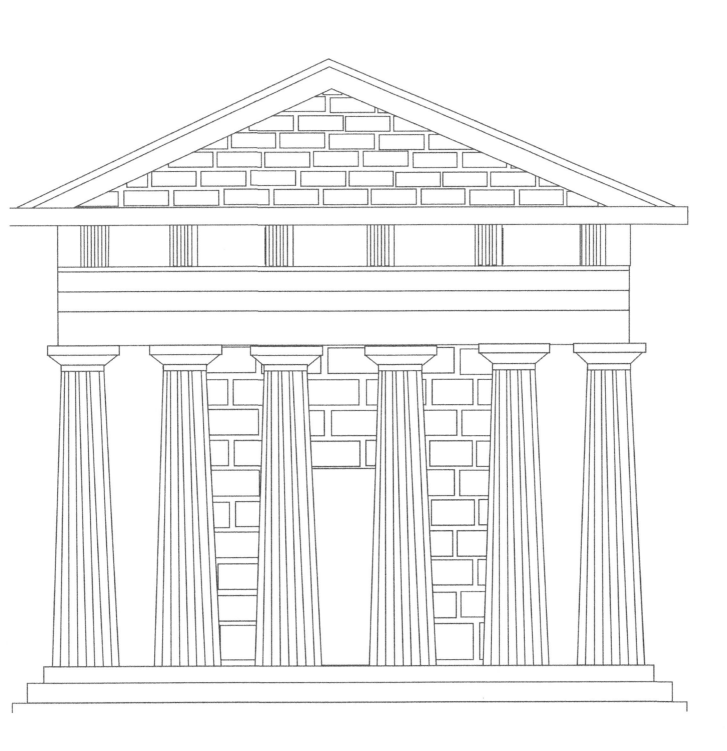

Romanesque style in architecture

Romanesque style in architecture (detail)

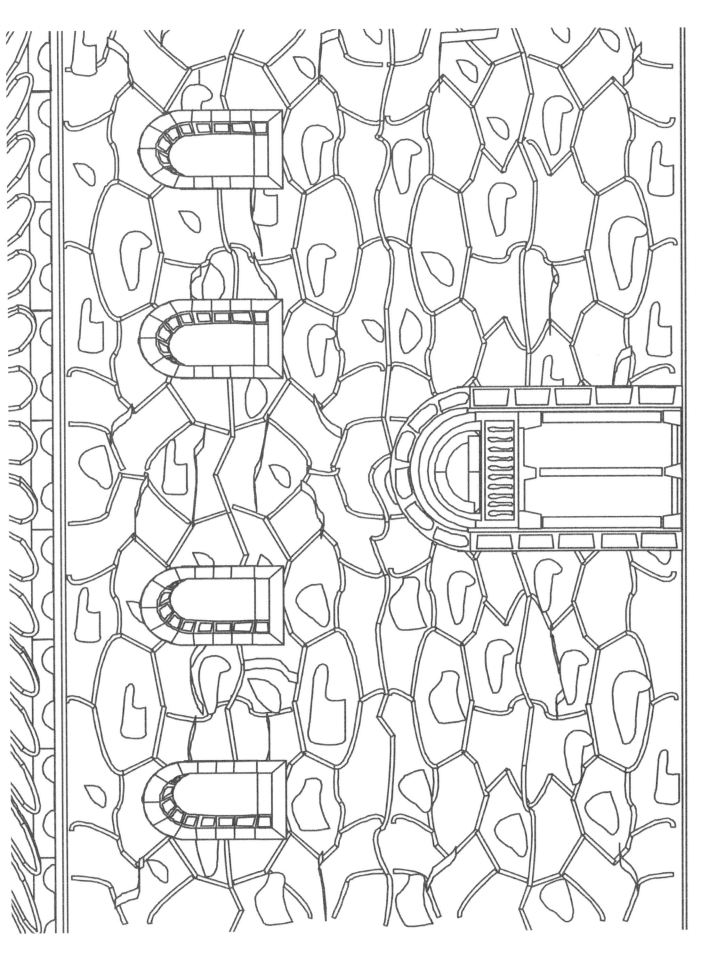

Gothic style in architecture

Gothic style in architecture
(detail)

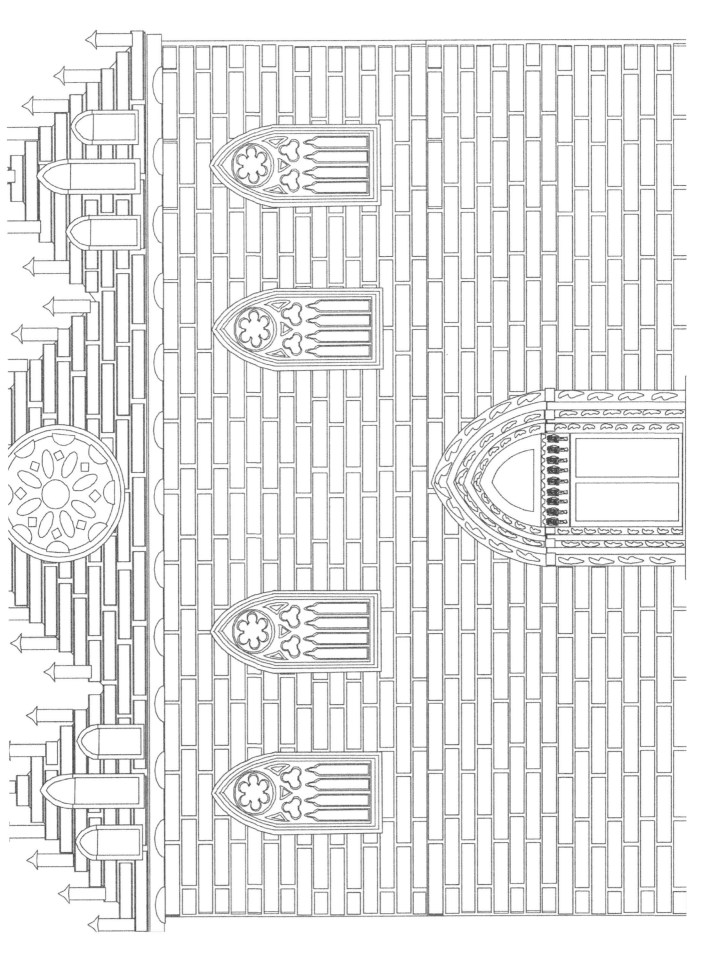

Renaissance style in architecture

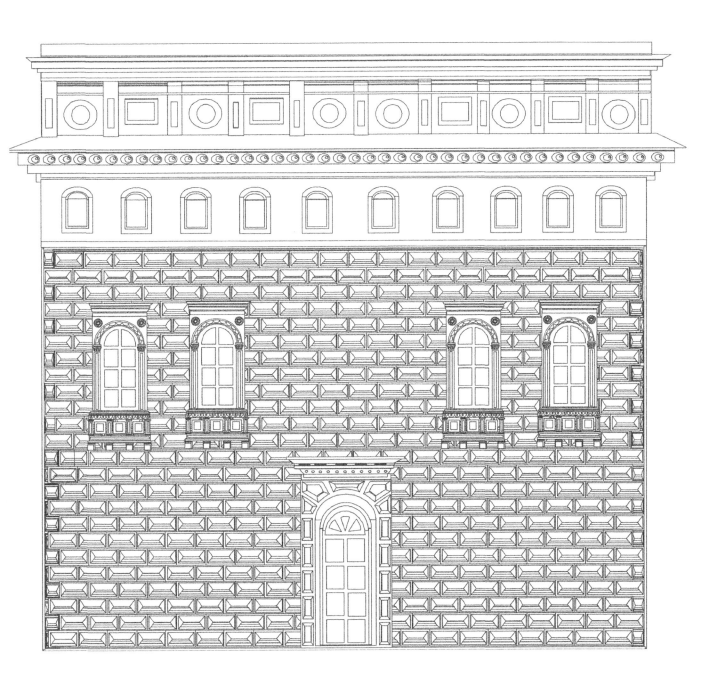

Renaissance style in architecture (detail)

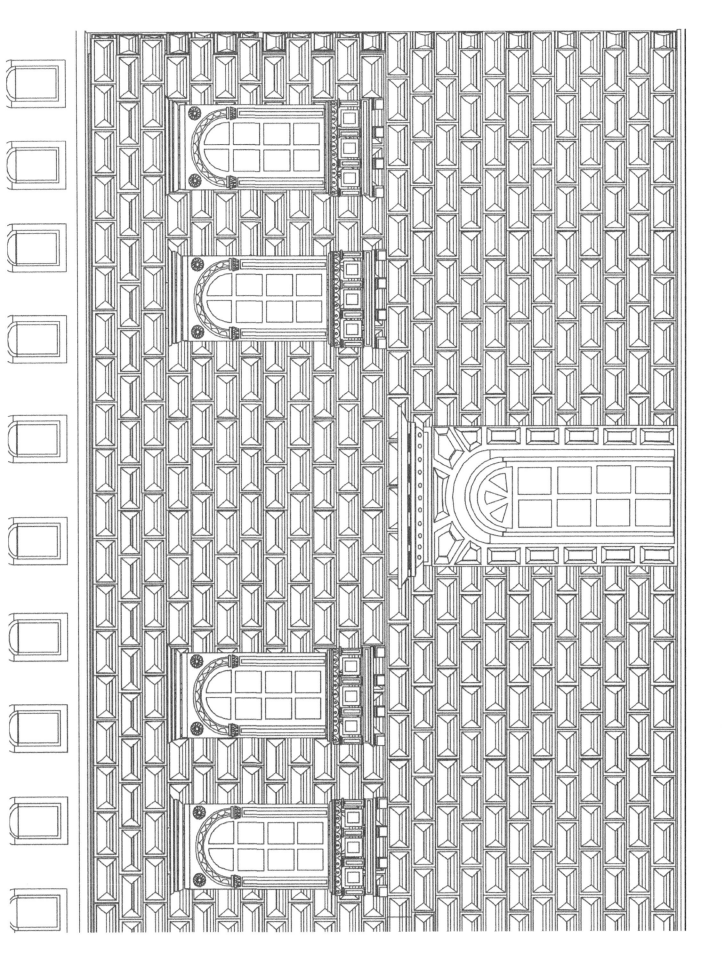

Baroque style in architecture

Baroque style in architecture
(detail)

Contemporary style in architecture

I Love Liberty (Roy Lichtenstein)

Tenements

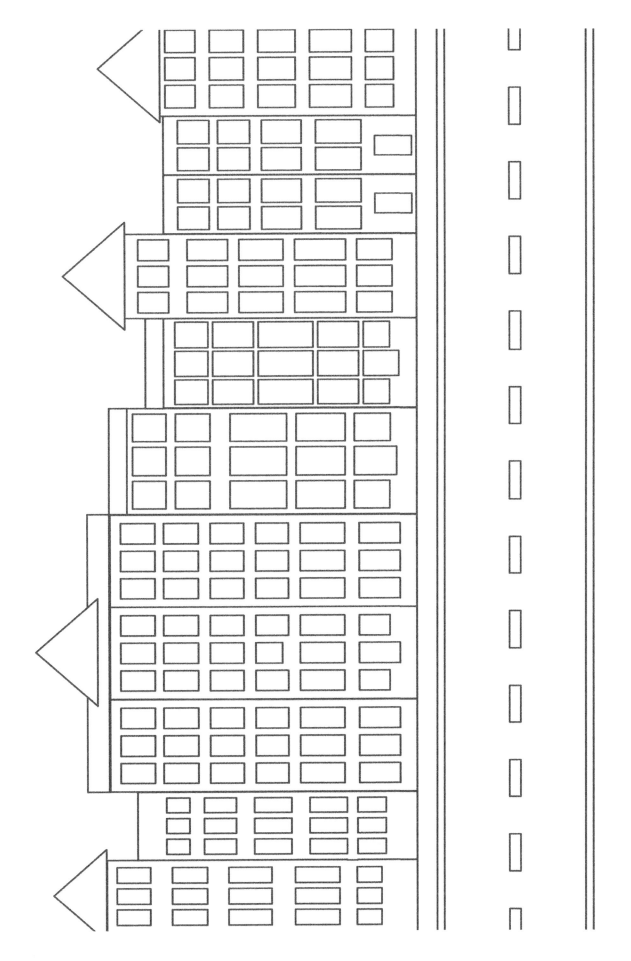

Old Town (Jordanow)

chrysler building

ONE WAY

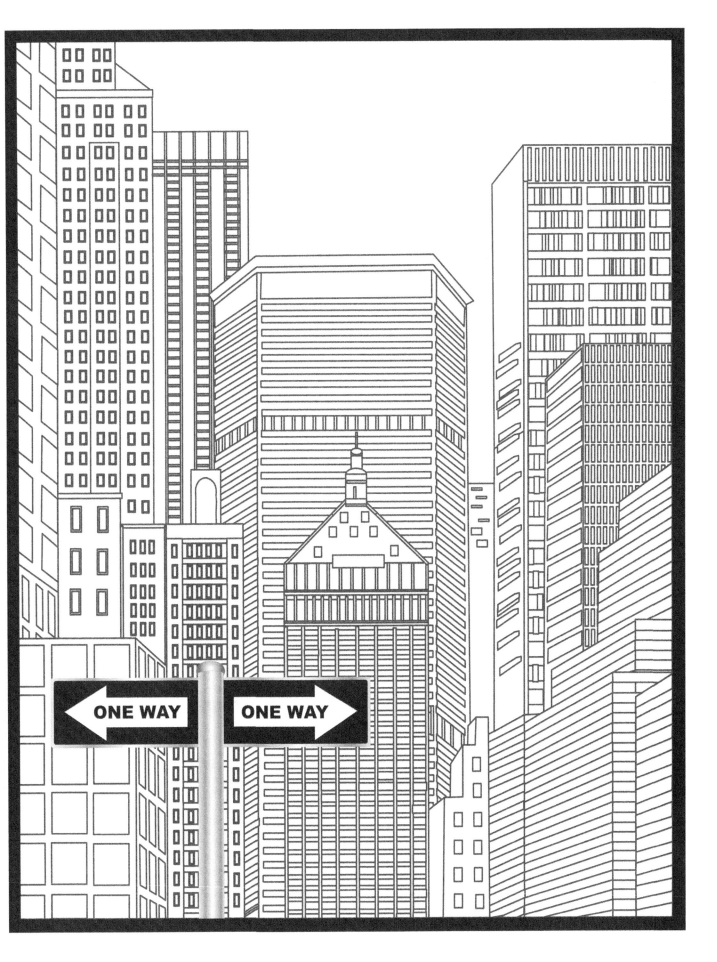

Bridge in Venice

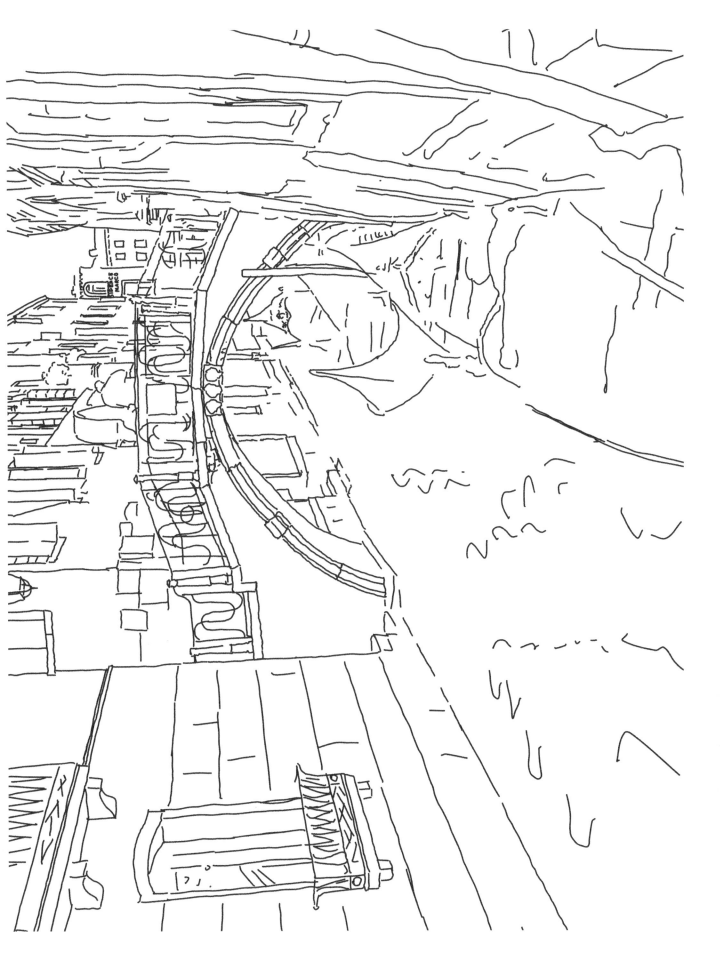

venice window

Canal Venice

Hotel Cavalletto

Hundertwasserhaus in Vienna

This Must Be The Place (Roy Lichtenstein)

Picture XVI. The Great Gate of Kiev

Wassily Kandynsky

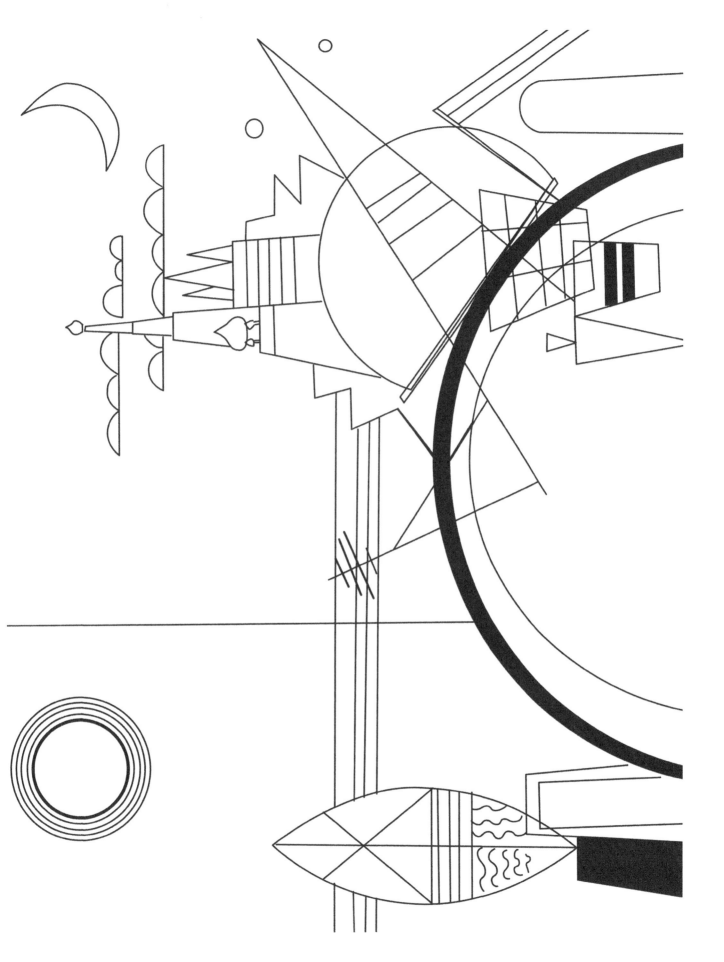

The yellow bridge at Ceret
Auguste Herbin

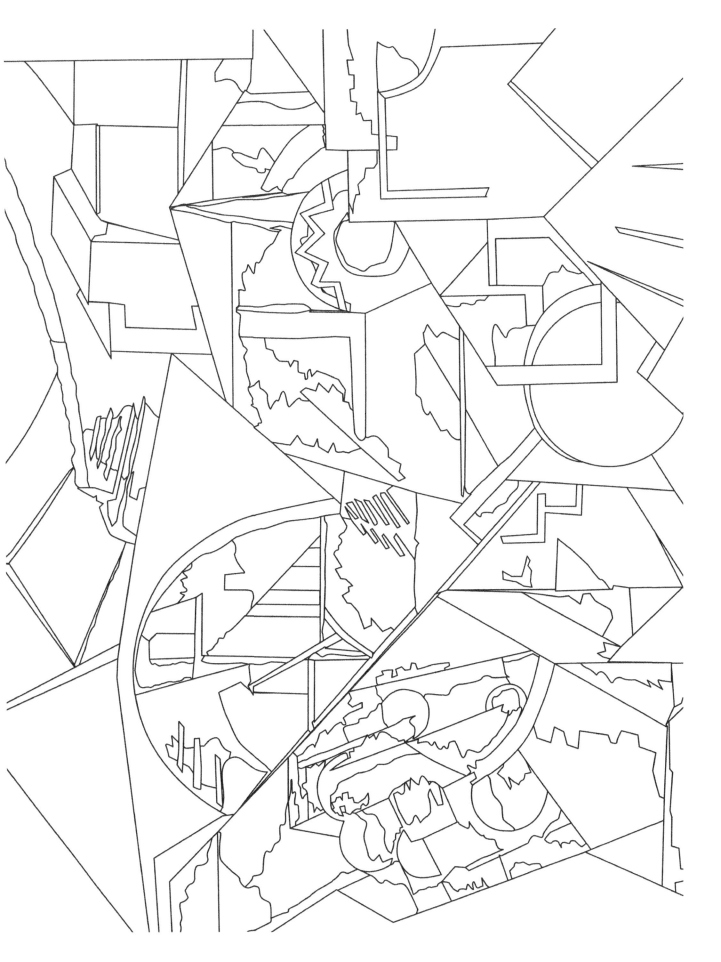

City Picture with Red and Green Accents

Paul Klee

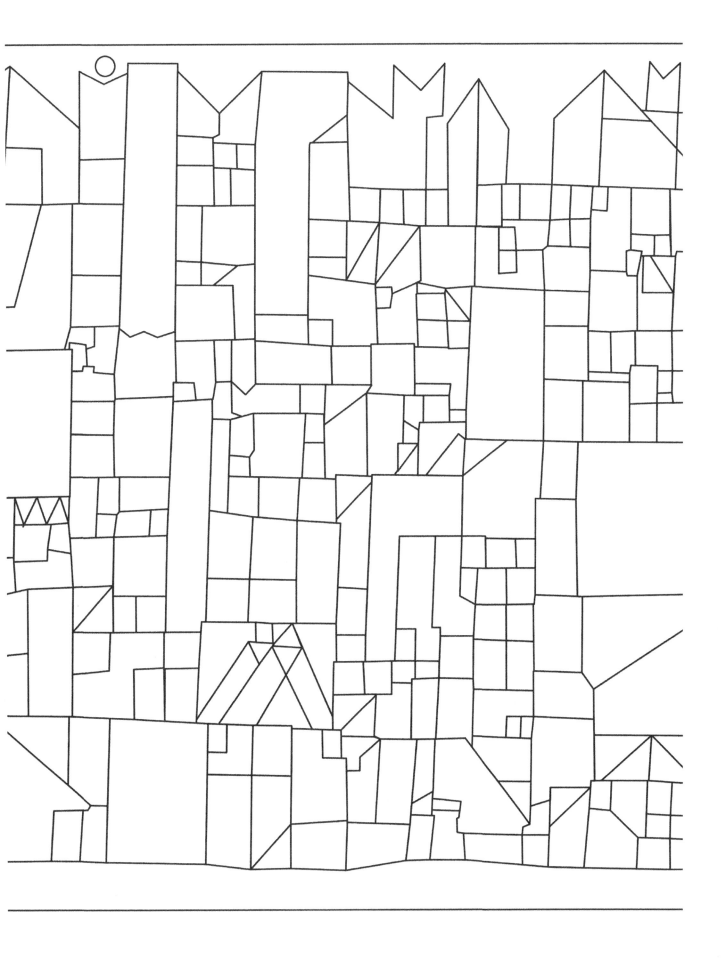

Workshop
Wyndham Lewis

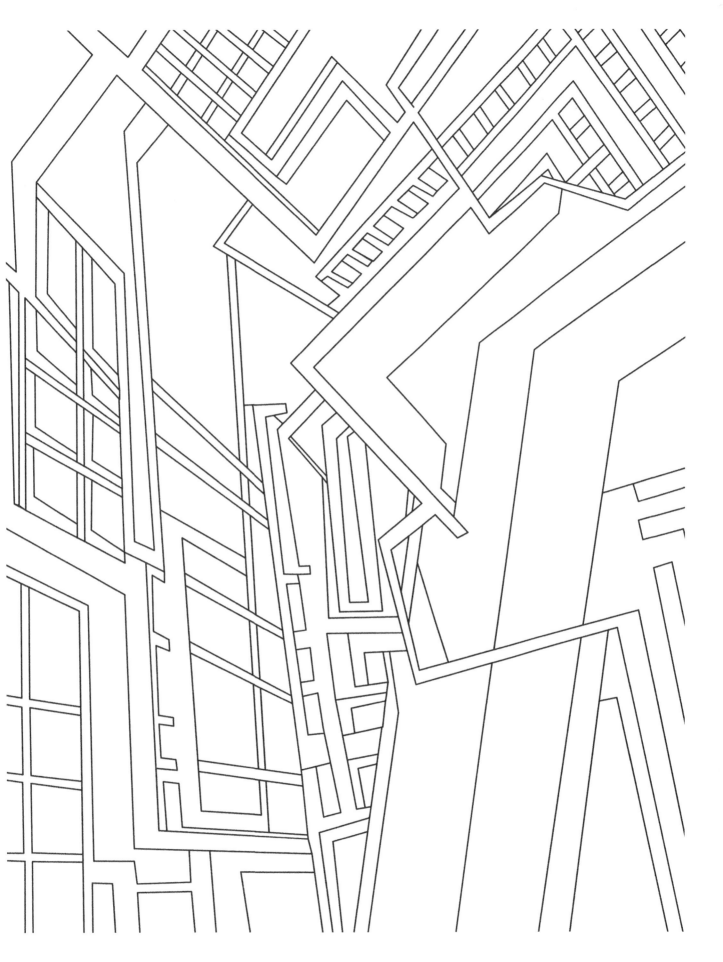

New York (Roy Lichtenstein)

Houses at Unterach on the Attersee

Gustav Klimt

Malcesine on Lake Garda

Gustav Klimt

Copyright Architecture Coloring Book

autor, illustrator: Jacek Lasa,

Made in the USA
Monee, IL
21 July 2022